GREAT POTATO COOKBOOK

Consultant Editor:
Valerie I

H

HERM.
HOUSE

Contents

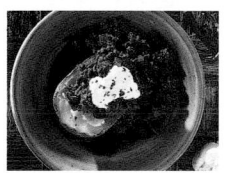
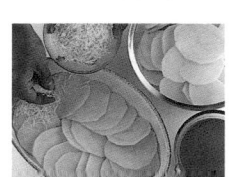

Introduction

The potato originated in South America. Sir Walter Raleigh is popularly credited with bringing potatoes to England from Virginia, but it is more likely that Sir Francis Drake, returning from the Caribbean in 1586, collected potatoes and tobacco when he provisioned his ships in Cartagena in northern Colombia. The first mention of potatoes in North America was not until 1719 in Londonderry, New Hampshire. They had been brought to the country by Irish settlers for whom they had already become a staple food and they have since spread to the rest of the world.

Nowadays, there are more than 400 varieties of potato, although only a handful are commonly seen in shops and supermarkets. Pre-packed potatoes are usually labelled, making it easy to choose the right variety for different recipes. They fall into two categories – new and maincrop or old. New potatoes are small and flavoursome and usually have white, firm-textured, waxy flesh. Maincrop and old potatoes can be subdivided into waxy and floury. The former are especially good for boiling, steaming and in salads, while the latter are perfect for baking, mashing and making into chips. Both may be used for roasting and frying.

Techniques

When preparing potatoes, use a peeler that removes only the very top surface, or scrub them, as most of the vitamins or minerals are contained in or just below the skin. Cook new and salad potatoes in their skins.

BAKING

1 Prick the skins and cook the potatoes at 160°C/325°F/Gas 3 for an hour or more for well browned and crunchy skins and fluffy flesh.

2 Besides simply mashing the flesh with butter and returning it to the skins, quick and easy fillings include grated cheese, cottage cheese, baked beans, chilli beans, canned tuna, prawns and mayonnaise, coleslaw, pesto sauce, and soured cream and chives.

3 Cook baked potatoes quickly in a microwave oven. Transfer to a hot oven for 10 minutes for a crisp skin.

BOILING

1 Cut the potatoes evenly (leave new ones whole), salt the water if liked, cover and cook over a moderate heat until they are soft. They can also be steamed in a steamer or colander.

2 Don't boil potatoes too fiercely; how long depends on variety. To test if they are ready, pierce carefully with a sharp knife.

CHIPS

1 Cut the potatoes into even-size sticks and remove excess starch by placing them in a large bowl of cold water for about 10 minutes before frying.

2 Drain the chips and dry them in a piece of muslin or an old dish towel before frying. The temperature of the oil should be at 190°C/375°F. Fry only as many chips as will comfortably sit in the oil.

3 When the chips are just beginning to colour, drain them and allow the oil to come back to temperature before plunging the chips back in. This browns the chips and means they don't soak up excessive amounts of oil.

MASHING

1 Boil the potatoes until tender, drain thoroughly and then tip them back into the pan.

2 Mash with a little milk and butter using a potato masher and season to taste with a little salt and pepper.

ROAST POTATOES

1 The best roast potatoes are made using a floury-textured potato. Peel and cut them into even-size chunks and par-boil them in lightly salted water until they begin to go tender and the outside looks soft.

2 Drain and then tip the potatoes back into the saucepan, put the lid on and shake the pan two or three times. This roughens up the surface.

3 Place the potatoes in a dish of hot oil or fat, and turn them over so that they are evenly coated.

4 Roast the potatoes in the oven at 220°C/425°F/Gas 7 for 40–50 minutes, until golden.

SAUTÉING

1 Peel potatoes thinly. Par-boil whole potatoes for 5–10 minutes, until they begin to soften. Drain them well and then slice into thick rounds.

2 Using sunflower oil or a mixture of sunflower and olive oil (butter will burn), fry the potatoes in a large frying pan. Turn occasionally and cook until evenly browned.

3 For diced potatoes, peel and cut into cubes, blanch for 2 minutes and drain. Fry in a little oil, turning.

STEAMING

1 Place potatoes on a bed of mint in a steamer or colander over a pan of boiling water for 15–20 minutes.

Potato Skewers with Mustard Dip

Potatoes cooked on the barbecue have a tasty flavour and crisp skin. These are served with a thick, garlic-rich dip.

Serves 4

INGREDIENTS

FOR THE POTATOES
1 kg/2¼ lb small new potatoes
200 g/7 oz/2 cups shallots, peeled and halved
30 ml/2 tbsp olive oil
15 ml/1 tbsp sea salt

FOR THE DIP
4 garlic cloves, crushed
2 egg yolks
30 ml/2 tbsp lemon juice
300 ml/½ pint/1¼ cups extra virgin olive oil
10 ml/2 tsp wholegrain mustard
salt and freshly ground black pepper

1 Par-boil the potatoes in boiling water for 5 minutes. Drain well and then thread them on to metal skewers with the shallots.

2 Brush with the olive oil and sprinkle with sea salt. Cook the potatoes and shallots for 10–12 minutes over a hot barbecue or under a preheated grill, turning the skewers occasionally, until tender.

3 To make the dip, place the crushed garlic, egg yolks and lemon juice in a blender or food processor and process for a few seconds until the mixture is smooth.

4 Keep the motor running and add the oil very gradually, pouring it in a thin stream, until the mixture forms a thick, glossy cream.

5 Add the mustard and season with salt and pepper to taste. Serve the potato skewers with the garlic dip.

Creole Potato Cheese Puffs

It's worth boiling extra potatoes just to have some left over to mash for this heartening and pretty starter.

Serves 4–6

INGREDIENTS
25 g/1 oz/2 tbsp butter, plus extra for
    greasing
45 ml/3 tbsp milk
450 g/1 lb/2½ cups cold mashed potatoes
50 g/2 oz/½ cup grated Cheddar cheese
4 spring onions, shredded
grated nutmeg
2 eggs, separated
salt and freshly ground black pepper
watercress and cherry tomatoes, to garnish

1 Preheat the oven to 220°C/425°F/ Gas 7 and generously grease a 12-hole non-stick bun tin, buttering the sections between the indents as well.

2 Warm the milk and butter to just below boiling point in a small pan, then mix thoroughly into the mashed potatoes, together with the cheese, spring onions, a pinch of nutmeg and salt and pepper to taste. Mix in the egg yolks and beat thoroughly.

3 Whisk the egg whites to soft peaks. Mix a tablespoon or two of the whites thoroughly into the potato mixture to loosen it, then fold the rest of the whites through the potato as lightly as you can.

4 Spoon the mixture into the bun tin and bake in the oven for about 15 minutes, until risen and golden brown. Serve immediately, garnished with watercress and cherry tomatoes.

COOK'S TIP: For a family supper, serve with sausages and ketchup.

Potato Latkes

Latkes, or pancakes, should be eaten whilst still piping hot and are sometimes served with hot salt beef or salami.

Serves 4

INGREDIENTS
2 medium potatoes
1 onion
1 large egg, beaten
30 ml/2 tbsp medium-ground
    matzo meal
oil, for frying
salt and freshly ground black pepper

1 Peel and coarsely grate the potatoes and the onion. Put them in a large colander, but don't rinse them. Press them down, squeezing out the thick starchy liquid with the back of a spoon. Alternatively, squeeze the mixture dry in a tea towel.

2 Immediately stir the beaten egg into the drained potato and onion mixture. Add the matzo meal, stirring well to mix. Season with salt and plenty of freshly ground black pepper.

3 Pour some oil into a frying pan to a depth of about 1 cm/½ in. Heat the oil for a few minutes (test it by throwing in a small piece of bread, which should sizzle).

4 Take a spoonful of the *latke* mixture and lower it carefully into the hot oil. Continue adding spoonfuls of the mixture, not too close together, over the base of the pan.

5 Flatten the pancakes slightly with the back of a spoon and after a few minutes, when the *latkes* are golden brown on one side, carefully turn them over. Continue frying until the other side is golden brown. Take care that they do not burn.

6 Remove the *latkes* from the pan and drain on kitchen paper. Transfer to a warm serving dish and serve immediately.

Spicy Potato Wedges with Chilli Dip

Try these healthy dry-roasted potato wedges. The crisp spice crust makes them irresistible, especially when served with a chilli dip.

Serves 2

INGREDIENTS
2 baking potatoes, about 225 g/8 oz each
30 ml/2 tbsp olive oil
2 garlic cloves, crushed
5 ml/1 tsp ground allspice
5 ml/1 tsp ground coriander
15 ml/1 tbsp paprika, plus extra to garnish
salt and freshly ground black pepper

FOR THE CHILLI DIP
15 ml/1 tbsp olive oil
1 small onion, finely chopped
1 garlic clove, crushed
200 g/7 oz can chopped tomatoes
1 fresh red chilli, seeded and finely chopped
15 ml/1 tbsp balsamic vinegar
15 ml/1 tbsp chopped fresh coriander, plus
    extra to garnish

1 Preheat the oven to 200°C/400°F/ Gas 6. Cut the baking potatoes in half, then cut each half into 4 wedges. Leave the skins on.

2 Place the wedges in a saucepan of cold water. Bring the water to the boil, then lower the heat and simmer gently for 10 minutes, or until the potato wedges have softened slightly. Drain the wedges well and pat them dry on kitchen paper.

3 Mix the oil, garlic, allspice, coriander and paprika in a roasting tin. Add salt and pepper to taste. Add the potatoes to the pan and shake to coat them thoroughly. Roast for 20 minutes, turning the potato wedges occasionally, or until they are browned, crisp and fully cooked.

4 Meanwhile, make the dip. Heat the oil in a saucepan, add the onion and garlic and cook for 5–10 minutes, until soft. Add the tomatoes and juice. Stir in the chilli and vinegar.

5 Cook gently for 10 minutes, until the mixture has reduced and thickened, then check the seasoning. Stir in the fresh coriander and serve hot, with the potato wedges. Garnish with salt, paprika and fresh coriander.

Potato & Gammon Broth

For extra colour, a few onion skins can be added when cooking the gammon, but remember to remove them before serving.

Serves 4

INGREDIENTS
450 g/1 lb gammon, in one piece
2 bay leaves
2 onions, sliced
10 ml/2 tsp paprika
675 g/1½ lb potatoes, cut into
  large chunks
225 g/8 oz spring greens
425 g/15 oz can haricot or cannellini
  beans, drained
salt and freshly ground
  black pepper

1 Soak the gammon overnight in plenty of cold water. Drain and place in a large saucepan with the bay leaves and the sliced onions. Pour over 1.5 litres/2½ pints/6¼ cups cold water.

2 Bring the water to the boil, then reduce the heat and allow the water to simmer very gently for about 1½ hours, until the gammon is tender. Check the pan from time to time to make sure the water doesn't boil over.

COOK'S TIP: Bacon knuckles can be used instead of the gammon. The knuckle bones and the marrow they contain will give the juices a delicious flavour.

3 Drain the meat, reserving the cooking liquid, and leave to cool. Discard the skin and any fat from the gammon and cut the meat into small chunks. Return the chunks to the pan with the paprika, potatoes and enough cooking liquid just to cover. Simmer gently, covered, for 20 minutes.

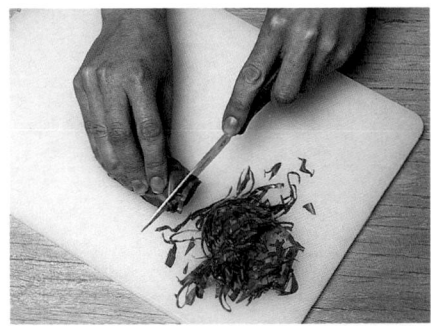

4 Cut away the stems from the greens. Roll up the leaves and cut into thin shreds. Add to the pan, together with the beans, and simmer for about 10 minutes. Season with salt and pepper to taste and serve hot.

Cold Potato & Leek Soup

Also called Vichyssoise, this flavourful soup is served with a swirl of crème fraîche or soured cream and sprinkled with a few snipped fresh chives.

Serves 6–8

INGREDIENTS
450 g/1 lb potatoes (about 3 large), peeled and cubed
1.5 litres/2½ pints/6¼ cups chicken stock
350 g/12 oz/4 medium leeks, trimmed
150 ml/¼ pint/⅔ cup crème fraîche or soured cream
salt and freshly ground black pepper
45 ml/3 tbsp snipped fresh chives, to garnish

1 Put the cubes of potato and the chicken stock in a saucepan or flameproof casserole and bring to the boil. Reduce the heat and allow to simmer for 15–20 minutes.

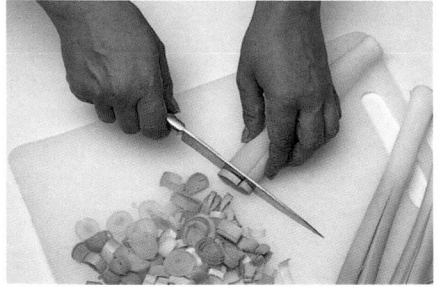

2 With a sharp knife, make a slit along the length of each leek and rinse well between all the layers under cold running water. Drain and cut the leeks into thin slices.

3 When the potatoes are barely tender, stir in the leeks. Season with salt and pepper and simmer for 10–15 minutes, until the vegetables are soft, stirring occasionally. If the soup appears too thick, thin it down with a little more stock or water.

4 Purée the soup in a blender or food processor, in batches if necessary. If you prefer a smoother soup, pass it through a food mill or press through a strainer. Stir in most of the cream, cool and chill. To serve, ladle into chilled bowls and garnish with a swirl of cream and chives.

Potato & Courgette Tortilla

Wedges of this vegetable omelette make a mouth-watering snack.

Serves 4

INGREDIENTS
450 g/1 lb potatoes, peeled and diced
30 ml/2 tbsp olive oil
1 onion, finely chopped
1 garlic clove, crushed
2 courgettes, thinly sliced
30 ml/2 tbsp chopped fresh tarragon
4 eggs, beaten
salt and freshly ground black pepper

1 Cook the potatoes in boiling, salted water for about 5 minutes. Drain.

2 Heat the oil in a large frying pan that can be used under the grill. Add the onion and cook gently for 3–4 minutes, until starting to soften. Add the potatoes, garlic and courgettes. Cook for about 5 minutes, shaking the pan occasionally, until the courgettes are softened and the potatoes are lightly browned.

3 Stir the tarragon into the eggs and season. Pour over the vegetables and cook over a moderate heat until the underside is set. Preheat the grill. Grill the tortilla until the top is set. Cut into wedges and serve.

Chicken & Pesto Potato Jackets

Pesto gives a wonderful lift to baked potatoes as well as pasta.

Serves 4

INGREDIENTS
4 baking potatoes, pricked
2 boned chicken breasts, with their skin on
250 ml/8 fl oz/1 cup low-fat natural yogurt
15 ml/1 tbsp pesto sauce
salt and freshly ground black pepper
fresh basil, to garnish

1 Preheat the oven to 200°C/400°F/ Gas 6. Bake the potatoes for about 1¼ hours, or until they are soft on the inside when tested with a knife.

2 About 20 minutes before the potatoes are ready, cook the chicken breasts. Either bake the breasts in a dish alongside the potatoes in the oven, or cook them on a rack under a moderately hot grill.

3 Stir together the yogurt, pesto and seasoning. When the potatoes are cooked through, cut them open. Skin and slice the chicken breasts. Fill the potatoes with the slices, top with yogurt and garnish with basil.

Right: Potato & Courgette Tortilla (top); Chicken & Pesto Potato Jackets.

Stuffed Potato Skins

Potato jackets filled with mildly spiced vegetables and topped with cheese.

Serves 6

INGREDIENTS
3 baking potatoes, about 350 g/12 oz each,
    scrubbed and patted dry
15 ml/1 tbsp vegetable oil
40 g/1½ oz/3 tbsp butter
1 onion, chopped
1 green pepper, seeded and coarsely chopped
5 ml/1 tsp paprika
115 g/4 oz/1 cup grated Cheddar or
    Monterey Jack cheese
salt and freshly ground black pepper
salad leaves and fresh parsley, to garnish

1 Preheat the oven to 200°C/400°F/
Gas 6. Brush the potatoes with oil
and prick on all sides. Bake until
tender, about 1½ hours.

2 Heat the butter in a non-stick
frying pan. Add the onion and a
little salt and cook over medium heat
for about 5 minutes until softened.
Add the pepper and cook for 2–3
minutes, until tender but crunchy. Add
the paprika and set aside.

3 When the baking potatoes are
done, cut them in half lengthways.
Scoop out the flesh with a spoon, but
try to keep the pieces of flesh fairly
coarse. Keep the potato skins warm.
Preheat the grill.

4 Add the potato flesh to the
ingredients in the frying pan and
cook over a high heat, stirring, until
the potato is lightly browned. Season
with freshly ground black pepper.

5 Divide the vegetable mixture
among the potato skins. Sprinkle
the cheese on top. Place under the
grill for 3–5 minutes, until the cheese
just melts. Serve the potato skins with
salad leaves and parsley sprigs.

COOK'S TIP: For Bacon-Stuffed
Potato Skins, add 115 g/4 oz/¾ cup
chopped cooked bacon to the
cooked potato flesh and vegetables.
Stuff as above.

Tex-Mex Baked Potatoes with Chilli

This is the perfect lunch for a cold winter's day – substantial and filling with a warm spicy kick.

Serves 4

INGREDIENTS
2 large baking potatoes
15 ml/1 tsp oil
1 garlic clove, crushed
1 small onion, chopped
½ small red pepper, seeded and chopped
225 g/8 oz lean minced beef
½ small fresh red chilli, seeded and chopped
5 ml/1 tsp ground cumin
pinch of cayenne pepper
200 g/7 oz can chopped tomatoes
30 ml/2 tbsp tomato purée
2.5 ml/½ tsp dried oregano
2.5 ml/½ tsp dried marjoram
200 g/7 oz can red kidney beans, drained
15 ml/1 tbsp chopped fresh coriander
60 ml/4 tbsp soured cream
salt and freshly ground black pepper
chopped fresh parsley, to garnish

1 Preheat the oven to 220°C/425°F/ Gas 7. Rub the potatoes with a little oil and pierce with skewers. Bake them on the top shelf for 30 minutes before beginning to cook the chilli.

2 Heat the oil in a pan and add the garlic, onion and pepper. Fry gently for 4–5 minutes, until softened.

3 Add the beef and fry until browned all over, then stir in the red chilli, cumin, cayenne pepper, tomatoes, tomato purée, 60 ml/4 tbsp water and the herbs. Cover and simmer for about 25 minutes, stirring occasionally.

4 Remove the lid, stir in the kidney beans and cook for 5 minutes. Turn off the heat and stir in the chopped coriander. Season well and set aside.

5 Halve the potatoes and place in bowls. Top with the chilli and soured cream. Garnish with parsley.

Hash Browns

A traditional American breakfast dish, hash browns can be served at any time of day. They are a tasty way of using up left-over boiled potatoes.

Serves 4

INGREDIENTS
60 ml/4 tbsp sunflower or olive oil
about 450 g/1 lb/3 cups diced, cooked
    potatoes
1 small onion, chopped
salt and freshly ground black pepper

1 Heat the oil in a large, heavy-based frying pan and when quite hot, add the potatoes in a single layer. Scatter the onion on top and season well.

2 Cook on a moderate heat until browned underneath, pressing down on the potatoes with a spoon or spatula to squash them together.

3 When the potatoes are nicely browned, turn them over in sections with a fish slice and fry on the other side, pressing them down once again until that side is brown too. Serve the hash browns when heated through and lightly crispy.

Pan Haggerty

Use a firm-fleshed potato, which will hold its shape when cooked. For a change, try adding chopped ham or salami.

Serves 2–4

INGREDIENTS
1 large onion
450 g/1 lb potatoes
30 ml/2 tbsp olive oil
25 g/1 oz/2 tbsp butter
2 garlic cloves, crushed
115 g/4 oz/1 cup grated mature
   Cheddar cheese
45 ml/3 tbsp chopped fresh chives, plus
   extra to garnish
salt and freshly ground black pepper

1 Peel, halve and slice the onion very thinly. Peel the potatoes, as close to the skin as possible, and cut into slices about 3 mm/⅛ in thick.

2 Heat the oil and butter in a large heavy-based or non-stick frying pan. Remove from the heat and cover the base with a layer of potatoes, followed by layers of onion, garlic, cheese, chives and seasoning.

3 Continue layering, ending with a layer of cheese. Cover the pan and cook over a gentle heat, for about 30 minutes, or until the potatoes and onion are tender.

4 Preheat the grill to hot. Uncover the pan, protect the pan handle with foil, and brown the top under the grill. Serve straight from the pan, sprinkled with extra chives to garnish.

Bacon & Herb Rösti

Grated potato is combined with bacon, onion and herbs to make a satisfying and deliciously crispy snack.

Serves 4

INGREDIENTS
450 g/1 lb medium potatoes, left whole and unpeeled
30 ml/2 tbsp olive oil, plus extra for greasing
1 red onion, finely chopped
4 lean back bacon slices, rinded and diced
15 ml/1 tbsp potato flour
30 ml/2 tbsp chopped fresh mixed herbs
salt and freshly ground black pepper
fresh parsley sprigs, to garnish

1 Lightly grease a baking sheet. Parboil the potatoes in a saucepan of lightly salted, boiling water for about 6 minutes. Drain the potatoes and set aside to cool slightly.

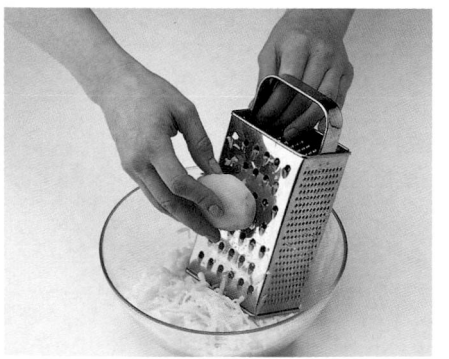

2 Once cool enough to handle, peel the potatoes and grate them into a bowl, using the coarse side of the grater. Set aside.

3 Heat 15 ml/1 tbsp of the olive oil in a frying pan, add the chopped onion and diced bacon and cook gently for 5 minutes, stirring occasionally to prevent sticking. Preheat the oven to 220°C/425°F/Gas 7.

4 Remove the pan from the heat. Stir the bacon and onion mixture, the remaining oil, potato flour, mixed herbs, salt and freshly ground black pepper into the grated potatoes and stir well to combine.

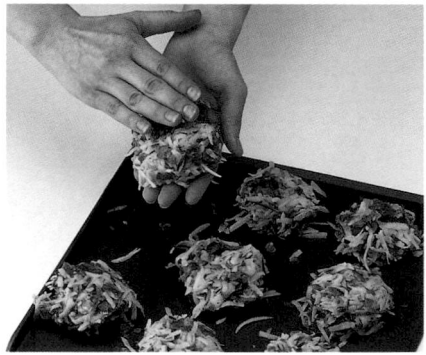

5 Divide the rösti mixture into eight small piles and use your hands to place them carefully on to the prepared baking sheet, leaving a little space between each one.

6 Bake for 20–25 minutes, until the rösti are crisp and golden brown. Serve immediately, garnished with sprigs of fresh parsley.

Potato & Spinach Galette

Creamy layers of potato, spinach and herbs make a warming and attractive vegetarian dish.

Serves 6

INGREDIENTS
900 g/2 lb large firm potatoes, peeled
450 g/1 lb fresh spinach
2 eggs
400 g/14 oz/1¾ cups low-fat cream cheese
15 ml/1 tbsp wholegrain mustard
50 g/2 oz chopped fresh herbs (e.g. chives, parsley, chervil or sorrel)
salt and freshly ground black pepper
mixed salad, to serve

1 Preheat the oven to 180°C/350°F/ Gas 4. Line a deep 23 cm/9 in cake tin with baking paper. In a pan, cover the potatoes with cold water. Bring to the boil, cook for 10 minutes and drain. Slice thinly when cooled.

2 Wash the spinach and place in a large pan with only the water that is clinging to the leaves. Cover and cook, stirring once, until just wilted. Drain well and squeeze out the excess moisture. Chop finely.

3 Beat the eggs with the cream cheese and mustard. Stir in the chopped spinach and fresh herbs.

4 Place a layer of the sliced potatoes in the tin, arranged in concentric circles. Top with a spoonful of the cheese mixture and spread out. Continue layering, seasoning as you go, ending with a layer of potatoes.

5 Cover the tin with foil and place in a roasting tin. Fill the roasting tin with enough boiling water to come halfway up the sides and cook in the oven for 45–50 minutes. Turn out and serve hot or cold with a mixed salad.

Potato, Spinach & Pine Nut Gratin

Pine nuts add a satisfying crunch to this gratin of wafer-thin potato slices and spinach in a creamy cheese sauce.

Serves 2–4

INGREDIENTS
450 g/1 lb potatoes
1 garlic clove, crushed
3 spring onions, thinly sliced
150 ml/¼ pint/⅔ cup single cream
250 ml/8 fl oz/1 cup milk
225 g/8 oz frozen chopped
    spinach, thawed
115 g/4 oz/1 cup grated Cheddar cheese
25 g/1 oz/¼ cup pine nuts
salt and freshly ground black pepper
lettuce and tomato salad,
    to serve (optional)

2 Scatter the crushed garlic and sliced spring onions evenly over the potatoes. Again, you may find it easier to use your fingers.

3 Pour the cream and milk over the potatoes, spring onion and garlic. Place the pan over a gentle heat, cover and cook for 8 minutes, or until the potatoes are tender.

4 Using both hands, squeeze the thawed spinach dry. Add the spinach to the potato mixture, stirring lightly to combine. Cover the pan and cook for 2 further minutes.

1 Peel the potatoes and cut them carefully into wafer-thin slices. Using your fingers, spread the slices out evenly in a large, heavy-based, non-stick frying pan, overlapping them slightly, as shown.

5 Add salt and freshly ground black pepper to taste, then carefully spoon the mixture into a gratin dish. Preheat the grill.

6 Sprinkle the grated cheese and pine nuts over the spinach and potato mixture. Heat the gratin under the grill for 2–3 minutes, until the topping is golden and bubbling.

COOK'S TIP: A simple lettuce and tomato salad makes a colourful accompaniment to this dish.

Potato Gnocchi with Gorgonzola Sauce

Gnocchi are prepared all over Italy with different ingredients used in different regions. These are *gnocchi di patate*, potato dumplings.

Serves 4

INGREDIENTS
450 g/1 lb floury potatoes unpeeled
1 large egg
115 g/4 oz/1 cup plain flour, plus extra
    for rolling
fresh thyme sprigs, to garnish
salt and freshly ground black pepper

FOR THE SAUCE
115 g/4 oz Gorgonzola cheese
60 ml/4 tbsp double cream
15 ml/1 tbsp fresh thyme,
    chopped
60 ml/4 tbsp freshly grated Parmesan
    cheese, to serve

1 Cook the potatoes in boiling salted water for about 20 minutes, until they are tender. Drain and, when cool enough to handle, remove the skins.

2 Press the potatoes through a strainer with the back of a spoon. Season and beat in the egg until completely incorporated.

3 Add the flour, a little at a time, stirring well with a wooden spoon after each addition, until you have a smooth dough. (You may not need all the flour.)

4 Turn the potato dough out on to a floured surface and knead for about 3 minutes, adding more flour if necessary. You are aiming for a smooth and soft dough that is not sticky to the touch.

5 Divide the dough into 6 equal pieces. Flour your hands and gently roll each piece of dough between your hands to form a log shape measuring 15–20 cm/6–8 in long and 2.5 cm/ 1 in diameter.

6 Cut each log shape into 6–8 pieces, about 2.5 cm/1 in long, then gently roll each piece in the flour. Form the logs into gnocchi by gently pressing each piece on to the floured surface with the tines of a fork. This will leave ridges in the dough.

7 To cook, drop about 12 gnocchi at a time into a large pan of boiling water. They should rise to the surface, after about 2 minutes. When this happens, cook for 4–5 minutes more. Remove and drain, and add the next batch as necessary.

8 Place the Gorgonzola, cream and thyme in a large frying pan and heat gently until the cheese melts, to form a thick, creamy consistency and to heat through. Add the drained gnocchi and toss well to combine. Serve with Parmesan and garnish with thyme.

Garlic Mashed Potatoes

Although there seems to be a lot of garlic in this dish, the flavour is sweet and subtle when cooked in this way.

Serves 6–8

INGREDIENTS
2 garlic bulbs, separated into cloves,
   unpeeled
115 g/4 oz/½ cup unsalted butter
1.5 kg/3½ lb baking potatoes, peeled and
   quartered
120–175 ml/4–6 fl oz/½–¾ cup milk
salt and freshly ground white pepper

1 Blanch the garlic cloves in boiling water for 2 minutes, then drain and peel. In a heavy frying pan, melt half the butter over a low heat.

2 Add the garlic cloves to the pan, cover and cook gently for 20–25 minutes, until the cloves are very tender and just golden, shaking the pan and stirring occasionally. Do not allow the garlic to scorch or brown. Remove the pan from the heat and allow to cool slightly.

3 Spoon the cooked garlic cloves and any remaining butter into a blender or a food processor and process until smooth.

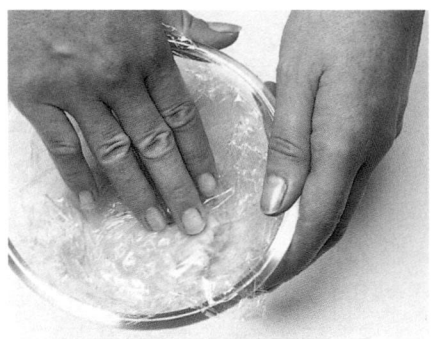

4 Tip the mixture into a small bowl, press clear film on to the surface to prevent a skin forming and set aside until the potatoes are cooked.

5 Put the potatoes in a large saucepan and add enough cold water just to cover. Add salt and bring to the boil over a high heat.

6 Cook the potatoes until they are tender, then drain and work through a food mill or use a potato masher and return to the pan.

7 Return the pan to medium heat and stir for 1–2 minutes to dry the potatoes completely. Remove the pan from the heat and keep warm.

8 Warm the milk over medium-high heat until bubbles start to form around the edge of the pan. Gradually beat the milk, remaining butter and reserved garlic purée into the potatoes and season with salt, if needed, and freshly ground white pepper. The dish makes the perfect accompaniment to all kinds of meats, especially roast or sautéed.

Scalloped Potatoes

These potatoes would make a delicious accompaniment to braised meat or a roast.

Serves 6

INGREDIENTS

1.2 kg/2½ lb potatoes, peeled and cut in
   3 mm/⅛ in slices
50 g/2 oz butter or margarine, cut in
   small pieces, plus extra for greasing
1 large onion, thinly sliced
25 g/1 oz/¼ cup plain flour
175 g/6 oz/1½ cups grated Cheddar cheese
200 ml/7 fl oz/scant 1 cup milk
475 ml/16 fl oz/2 cups single cream
salt and freshly ground black pepper

1 Preheat the oven to 180°C/350°F/
   Gas 4. Grease a 25 cm/10 in oval
gratin dish.

2 Make 4 layers each of the
   following: sliced potatoes and
onion, sprinkled flour, dots of butter
or margarine, seasoning and cheese.

3 Heat the milk and cream in a small
   saucepan. Pour the mixture evenly
over the potatoes.

4 Cover the gratin dish with foil and
   bake for 1 hour. Remove the foil
and bake for a further 15–20 minutes,
until the potatoes are tender and the
top is golden.

New Potatoes with Herbs

Serve these flavoursome potatoes with grilled chops or steak or with poached fish.

Serves 6

INGREDIENTS

500 g/1¼ lb small new potatoes
50 g/2 oz/4 tbsp butter or margarine
3 shallots or 1 small to medium onion,
   finely chopped
2 garlic cloves, peeled and crushed
5 ml/1 tsp chopped fresh tarragon
5 ml/1 tsp chopped fresh chives
5 ml/1 tsp chopped fresh parsley
salt and freshly ground black pepper

1 Bring a saucepan of salted water to
   the boil. Add the potatoes and
cook for 15–20 minutes until just
tender. Drain well.

2 Melt the butter or margarine in a
   frying pan. Add the shallots or
onion and garlic and cook over low
heat for about 5 minutes, until
softened. Add the potatoes, stir well
and season. Cook, stirring, until the
potatoes are heated through.

3 Transfer the potatoes to a warm
   serving bowl. Sprinkle with the
chopped herbs before serving.

*Right: Scalloped Potatoes (top);
New Potatoes with Herbs.*

Hasselback Potatoes

Crispy roast potatoes are coated in an orange glaze and returned to the oven until they are deep golden brown and crunchy.

Serves 4–6

INGREDIENTS
4 large potatoes, peeled
25 g/1 oz butter, melted
45 ml/3 tbsp olive oil

FOR THE GLAZE
juice of 1 orange
grated rind of ½ orange
15 ml/1 tbsp demerara sugar
freshly ground black pepper

1 Preheat the oven to 190°C/375°F/Gas 5. Cut each potato in half lengthways, place flat side down and then cut down as if making very thin slices, but leaving the bottom 1 cm/½ in intact.

2 Place the potatoes in a large roasting tin. Brush them generously with the melted butter and pour the olive oil over the base and around the potatoes.

3 Bake the potatoes in the oven for 40–50 minutes, until they begin to brown. Baste them occasionally with the butter and oil during the cooking process.

4 Meanwhile, place the orange juice and rind, pepper and sugar in a saucepan and heat gently, stirring until the sugar has dissolved. Simmer for 3–4 minutes, until the glaze is fairly thick, and then remove from the heat.

5 When the potatoes begin to brown, brush with the glaze and return to the oven for a further 15 minutes, or until deep golden brown. Serve immediately.

Gratin Dauphinois

This rich and creamy dish is a good alternative to roast potatoes, and it needs no last-minute attention.

Serves 8

INGREDIENTS
butter, for greasing
1.75 kg/4–4½ lb potatoes
115 g/4 oz/1 cup grated
    Cheddar cheese
2–3 garlic cloves, crushed
2.5 ml/½ tsp grated nutmeg
600 ml/1 pint/2½ cups milk
300 ml/½ pint/1¼ cups single cream
2 large eggs, beaten
salt and freshly ground black pepper

1 Preheat the oven to 180°C/350°F/ Gas 4. Butter a 2.4 litre/4 pint/ 10 cup shallow ovenproof dish. Peel the potatoes and slice them thinly.

3 Whisk the milk, cream and eggs together and pour them evenly over the layered potatoes, making sure that the liquid goes all the way to the base of the dish.

2 Mix together two-thirds of the cheese, garlic and nutmeg and season well. Layer the potatoes in a dish, sprinkling the cheese mixture over each layer except the top one.

4 Scatter the remaining third of the cheese on top of the layers and bake the gratin for 45–50 minutes, or until the top is golden brown. Test the potatoes with a sharp knife; they should be very tender.

Bombay Spiced Potatoes

Serve these Indian potatoes with curries and strong meat dishes.

Serves 4

INGREDIENTS
4 large potatoes, diced
60 ml/4 tbsp sunflower oil
1 garlic clove, finely chopped
10 ml/2 tsp brown mustard seeds
5 ml/1 tsp black onion seeds (optional)
5 ml/1 tsp ground turmeric
5 ml/1 tsp ground cumin
5 ml/1 tsp ground coriander
5 ml/1 tsp fennel seeds
dash of lemon juice
salt and freshly ground black pepper
chopped fresh coriander and lemon wedges,
   to garnish

1 Add the potatoes to a pan of boiling salted water, simmer for about 4 minutes until just tender, and drain.

2 Heat the oil in a large frying pan and add the garlic and all the spices. Fry gently for 1–2 minutes, stirring, until the mustard seeds pop.

3 Add the potatoes and stir-fry over a moderate heat for about 5 minutes, until heated through and well coated.

4 Season and sprinkle with lemon juice. Garnish with coriander and lemon wedges.

Spanish Chilli Potatoes

Reduce the quantity of chilli in this Spanish *tapas* dish if you prefer.

Serves 4

INGREDIENTS
1 kg/2¼ lb new or salad potatoes
60 ml/4 tbsp olive oil
1 onion, finely chopped
2 garlic cloves, crushed
15 ml/1 tbsp tomato purée
200 g/7 oz can chopped tomatoes
15 ml/1 tbsp red wine vinegar
2–3 small dried red chillies, seeded and
   chopped finely, or 5–10 ml/1–2 tsp hot
   chilli powder
5 ml/1 tsp paprika
salt and freshly ground black pepper
fresh flat leaf parsley sprig,
   to garnish

1 Boil the potatoes in their skins for 10–12 minutes, or until just tender. Drain and cool, then cut in half.

2 Fry the onion and garlic in the oil. Add the remaining ingredients, except the potatoes, seasoning and parsley, and simmer for about 5 minutes.

3 Add the potatoes, cover and simmer gently for 10 minutes. Season well and garnish with parsley.

Right: Bombay Spiced Potatoes (top); Spanish Chilli Potatoes.

New Potato & Chive Salad

The secret of a good potato salad is to mix the potatoes with the dressing while they are still hot so that they absorb it.

Serves 4–6

INGREDIENTS
675 g/1½ lb new potatoes (unpeeled)
5 spring onions
45 ml/3 tbsp olive oil
15 ml/1 tbsp white wine vinegar
4 ml/¾ tsp Dijon mustard
175 ml/6 fl oz/¾ cup mayonnaise
45 ml/3 tbsp chopped fresh chives
salt and freshly ground black pepper

1 Cook the potatoes in boiling salted water until tender. Finely chop the white parts of the spring onions, together with a little green.

2 Whisk together the olive oil, white wine vinegar and Dijon mustard. Drain the potatoes well, then immediately toss lightly with the vinegar mixture and chopped spring onions and leave to cool.

3 Stir the mayonnaise and chopped chives into the potatoes and chill well, covered, until ready to serve.

COOK'S TIP: Look out for the small, waxy potatoes sold especially for salads and cold dishes – they are particularly good in this recipe.

Potato Watercress Salad Bowl

New potatoes are equally good hot or cold, and this colourful, nutritious salad is an ideal way of making the most of them.

Serves 4

INGREDIENTS
450 g/1 lb small new potatoes, unpeeled
1 bunch watercress, torn in pieces
200 g/7 oz/1½ cups cherry tomatoes, halved
30 ml/2 tbsp pumpkin seeds
45 ml/3 tbsp fromage frais
15 ml/1 tbsp cider vinegar
5 ml/1 tsp light brown sugar
salt and paprika

1 Cook the potatoes in lightly salted, boiling water until just tender, then drain and leave to cool.

2 Toss together the potatoes, watercress, tomatoes and pumpkin seeds in a salad bowl.

3 Place the fromage frais, cider vinegar, sugar and salt and paprika to taste, in a screwtop jar and shake well to mix thoroughly. Pour the dressing over the salad just before you are ready to serve.

COOK'S TIP: If you are packing this salad for a picnic, take the dressing in the jar and toss in just before serving.

Curried New Potato & Green Bean Salad

Tender new potatoes and green beans tossed together in a subtly flavoured light dressing make a delicious salad.

Serves 6

INGREDIENTS
225 g/8 oz/1½ cups green beans, trimmed and halved
675 g/1½ lb cooked baby new potatoes
2 bunches spring onions, chopped
115 g/4 oz/⅔ cup sultanas
75 g/3 oz ready-to-eat dried pears, finely chopped
90 ml/6 tbsp reduced-calorie mayonnaise
60 ml/4 tbsp low fat plain yogurt
30 ml/2 tbsp Greek yogurt
15 ml/1 tbsp tomato purée
15 ml/1 tbsp curry paste
30 ml/2 tbsp snipped fresh chives
salt and freshly ground black pepper

2 Put the potatoes, beans, spring onions, sultanas and pears in a bowl and mix together.

3 In a small bowl, mix together the mayonnaise, yogurts, tomato purée, curry paste, chives and seasoning.

1 Cook the green beans in boiling water for about 5 minutes, until tender. Rinse under cold running water, drain well and set aside.

4 Add the dressing to the bowl and toss the ingredients together to mix. Cover and leave to stand for at least 1 hour before serving.

Index

This edition published by Hermes House

Hermes House is an imprint of
Anness Publishing Limited
Hermes House, 88–89 Blackfriars Road, London SE1 8HA

Publisher: Joanna Lorenz
Editor: Valerie Ferguson
Series Designer: Bobbie Colgate Stone
Designer: Andrew Heath
Editorial Reader: Joy Wotton
Production Controller: Joanna King
Recipes contributed by: Catherine Atkinson,
Angela Boggiano, Carla Capalbo, Frances Cleary,
Carole Clements, Roz Denny, Matthew Drennan,
Sarah Edmonds, Joanna Farrow, Christine France,
Silvano Franco, Sarah Gates, Christine Ingrams,
Judy Jackson, Ruby Le Bois, Lesley Mackley,
Norma MacMillan, Sue Maggs, Maggie Pannell,
Anne Sheasby, Hilaire Walden, Laura Washburn,
Jeni Wright
Photography: William Adams-Lingwood, Karl Adamson,
Steve Baxter, James Duncan, Michelle Garrett,
John Heseltine, Amanda Heywood, Janine Hosegood,
David Jordan, Don Last, Patrick McLeavey,
Michael Michaels, Thomas Odulate

© Anness Publishing Limited 1999, updated 2000
2 3 4 5 6 7 8 9 10

Notes:
For all recipes, quantities are given in both metric and
imperial measures and, where appropriate, measures
are also given in standard cups and spoons.
Follow one set, but not a mixture, because they are
not interchangeable.

Standard spoon and cup measures are level.
1 tsp = 5 ml   1 tbsp =15 ml
1 cup = 250 ml/8 fl oz

Australian standard tablespoons are 20 ml.
Australian readers should use 3 tsp in place of 1 tbsp
for measuring small quantities of gelatine, cornflour,
salt, etc.

Medium eggs are used unless otherwise stated.

Printed and bound in China